How to Draw
Flowers

Written and Illustrated by
Janice Kinnealy

Watermill Press

Basic Shapes

Here are the basic shapes you will need to draw the flowers in this book. Some will be familiar to you:

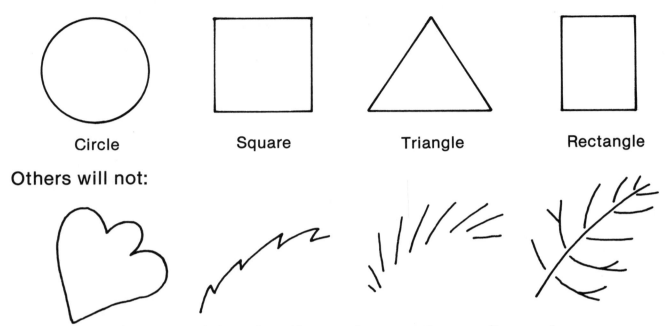

Circle   Square   Triangle   Rectangle

Others will not:

After you've practiced drawing these shapes, draw a flower for someone you love!

MATERIALS

Tracing paper   Drawing paper

Crayons   Pencils   Eraser

Introduction

Flowers are fun to draw! Each of the drawings in this book is shown in several simple steps. Just follow each step, and you'll add to your drawing as you go along. Soon you'll have a beautiful bouquet of flowers!

Before you begin, you may want to trace over some of the steps. This will give you an idea of how to put together the basic shapes for each flower. When your flower looks the way you want it to, color it with crayons.

Remember, the best part of your drawing is what *you* add to it with a little imagination. Draw several kinds of flowers. Then mix and match them to form your own bouquet. You may even want to spray them with a little perfume for a scented effect!

Here are the parts of a flower:

Petal (the pretty part that catches our eye)

Pistil (the part that makes the seeds)

Stamen (the part that holds the pollen)

Sepal (the cup that holds the petals together)

Tulip

Take a trip in your imagination to a faraway place. You're in Holland! What do you see? Windmills, wooden shoes, silver skates, and—tulips!

Tulips are the most popular of all bulb plants. There are hundreds of varieties and they come in just about every color—there's even a tulip with green petals! Tulips should be planted in late autumn to bloom the following spring.

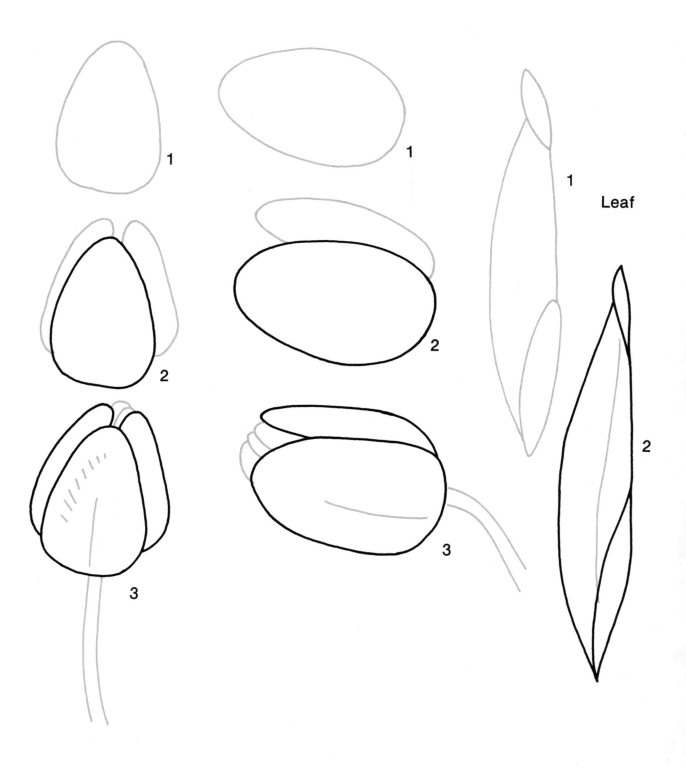

The name *tulip* comes from a word that means "turban." Look at the tulip flower. Can you see its resemblance to the turban hat?

(Turn to page 7 for directions on how to draw a bulb.)

Daffodil

Daffodils are the trumpeters of spring! Long before leaves appear on the trees, these colorful yellow flowers brighten the countryside like a burst of sunshine.

Some daffodils stand only a few inches tall, while others are more than two feet tall. Their colors can be white, cream, or yellow.

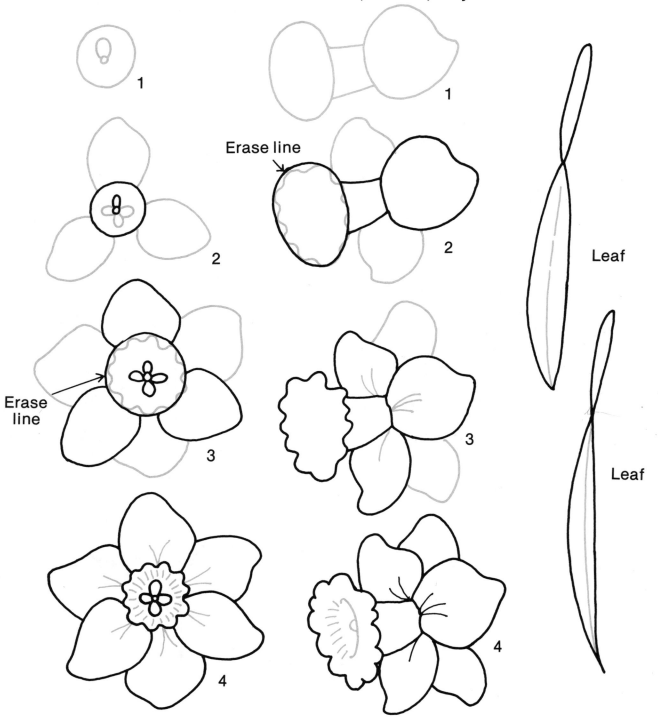

Daffodil bulbs are usually planted in the grass or beneath trees or shrubs.

The best-known of the daffodils is the "trumpet narcissus." It has one blossom at the end of each stalk. Look at the picture of the trumpet narcissus below. Can you tell how it got its name?

1

2

Bulb

3

Petunia

Petunias are a favorite garden plant prized for their large, velvety, funnel-shaped flowers. Petunias grow from early summer until the first frost. They are planted in masses and may be grown from cuttings or from seeds. For a ticklish surprise, run your finger along the petals of a petunia —they're covered with tiny hairs!

1

2

3

4

Erase line

5

Marigold

Marigolds grow in an astonishing assortment of colors, shapes, and sizes from the six-inch dwarf to the three-foot giant! The marigold is known for its hardiness—it can grow and bloom with little attention. So, if you *don't* have a green thumb, this may be the flower for you!

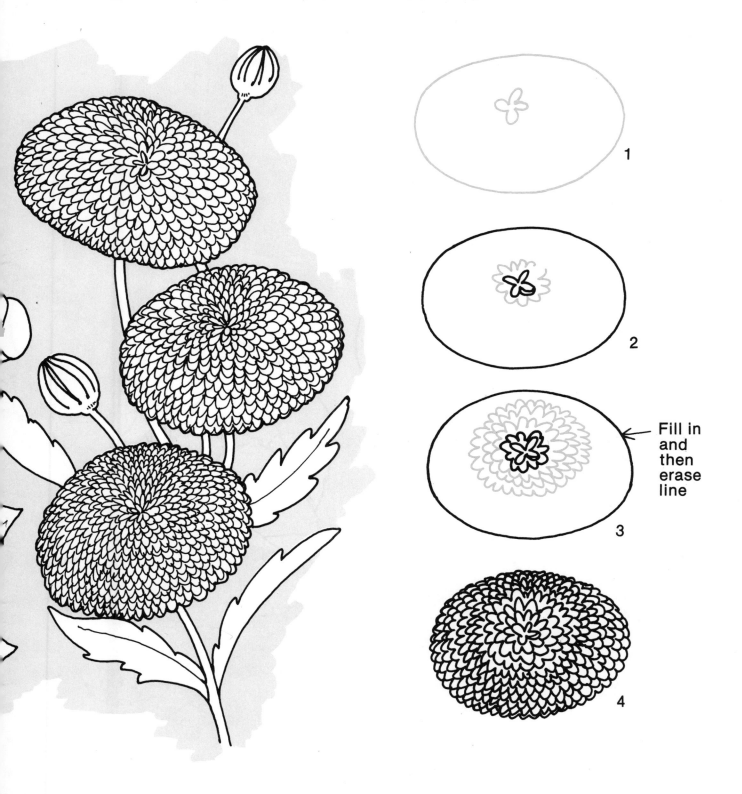

1

2

Fill in
and
then
erase
line

3

4

Violet

Violets are the most abundant of all spring flowers, growing in fields, woodlands, and even along roadsides. The flower varies in color from deep purple and blue to yellow and white. With over 100 species in the United States alone, the violet is the official state flower of four different states. Can you name them?

(Turn the page upside down for the answer.)

Leaf

1

Erase
line

1

2

3

4

5

3

Chrysanthemum

Chrysanthemums are among the most popular of all flowers because they are so long-lasting! They grow in the shorter daylight hours of autumn and may be grown in greenhouses too, if the amount of light is controlled. Long ago, the chrysanthemum was the favorite flower of Japanese emperors. Today the Feast of the Chrysanthemums is still celebrated in Japan!

1

2

Erase line

Fill in

3

4

Leaf

1

2

Erase line

3

SEEDS

Sunflower

It's easy to see how the sunflower got its name. With its sunlike flower head surrounded by "rays" of yellow petals, the sunflower looks kind of sunny!

Long ago, in Mexico, images of the sunflower were hammered out of pure gold and worshipped in the temples of the Aztec Indians!

Fill in

1

2

Leaf

Fill up
outer edge
with
petals

3

Today, this large, beautiful flower can be used for a number of purposes. Farmers grow sunflowers for seeds. The seeds can be crushed to make cooking oil and feed for cattle and poultry. Sunflower seeds are also sold as food for people. Have you ever tasted a sunflower seed?

Rose

The rose is a symbol of fragrance and loveliness. Roses come in many colors including pink, red, yellow, and white. The most popular of the garden roses is the *hybrid,* or flower bred from two varieties of roses. Roses need several hours of sunlight, well-drained soil, and protection from cold winds in order to grow.

Wild Rose

The wild rose is a prickly shrub that spring turns into a beautiful bouquet of pink blossoms. The flower is later replaced by fruits, called *hips,* which are used to make jellies and other foods.

Leaves

1

2

3

4

Wild Pansy

The wild pansy is a hardy little plant that's easy to grow! It is commonly found in parks and gardens and is easy to identify by the combination of colors on its petals—yellow, white, violet, and blue.

Daisy

Daisies are actually wild chrysanthemums, or weeds. The daisy got its name from the two words *day's eye*. Look at the picture of the daisy below. Can you tell how it got its name? (Hint: Daisies open their blossoms in the morning and close them at night.)

Leaf

Erase line

1

2

3

Foxgloves

Foxgloves are tall, branching plants that grow in open woodland areas. They have large, yellow, tubelike flowers with leaves on the opposite sides. When dried, the leaves are used to make a medicine for the heart.

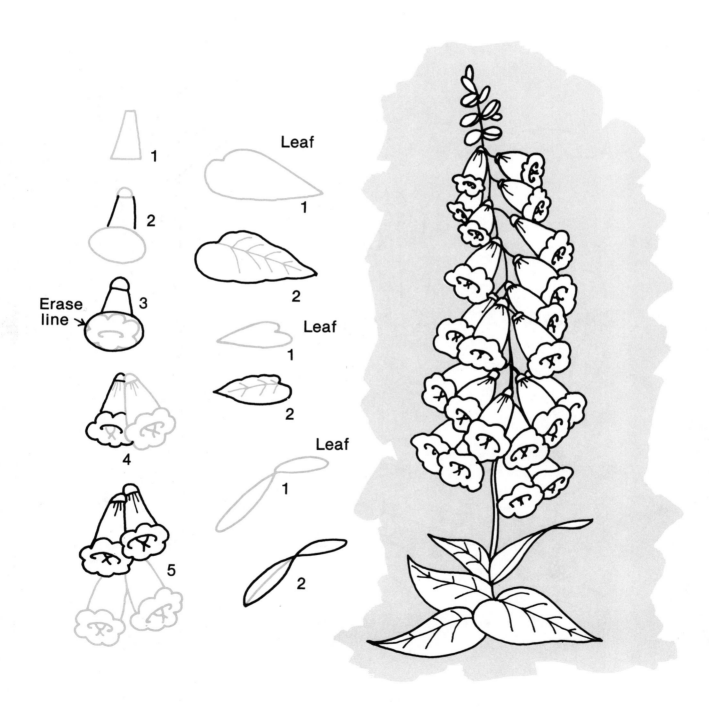

Leaf

Erase line →

Leaf

Leaf

Queen Anne's Lace

Queen Anne's Lace is actually a carrot that grows wild! Above ground, the plant is a lacy cluster of small white flowers with a single dark purple flower at its center. Look at the picture of Queen Anne's Lace below. Can you tell how it got its name?

1

2

← Erase line

Fill in

3

4

Dandelion

Dandelions are bright yellow wild flowers that grow in lawns and meadows. Gardeners dig deep into the ground to rid their lawns of these pesty weeds. But dandelions can be useful little plants!

Young dandelion leaves can be used in salads, and they can be cooked. They also make an excellent honey, according to an old recipe!

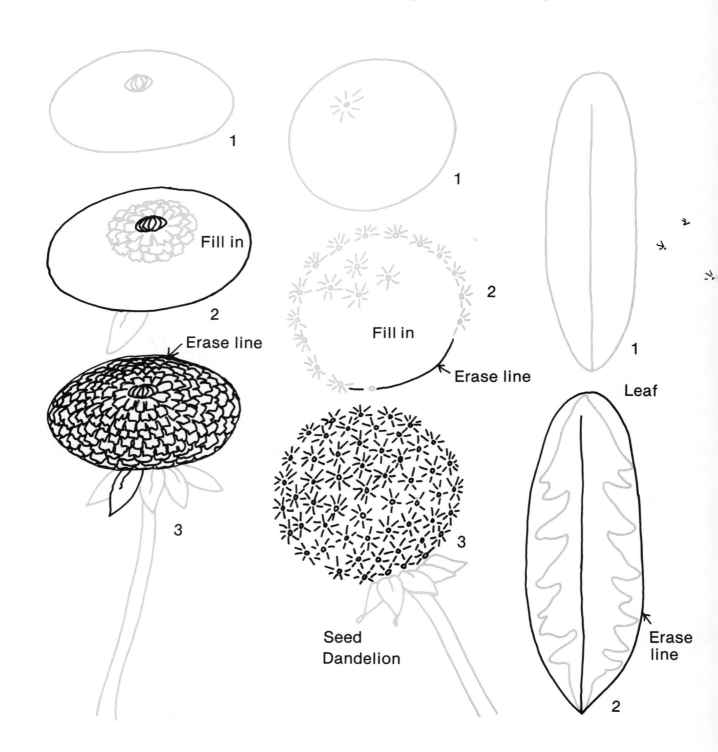

Fill in

Erase line

Fill in

Erase line

Seed
Dandelion

Leaf

Erase line

When they have finished flowering, dandelions can be lots of fun. Filmy wisps of hair, called *achene,* form. The achene is so light that it can be blown far and wide by the wind. Children often make a game of blowing achene from the dandelion stem—try it, sometime, when your neighbors aren't looking!

Flax

Flax is one of the oldest plants known. It has been used for centuries to make clothing. The next time you spread out a linen tablecloth, remember —it came from flax!

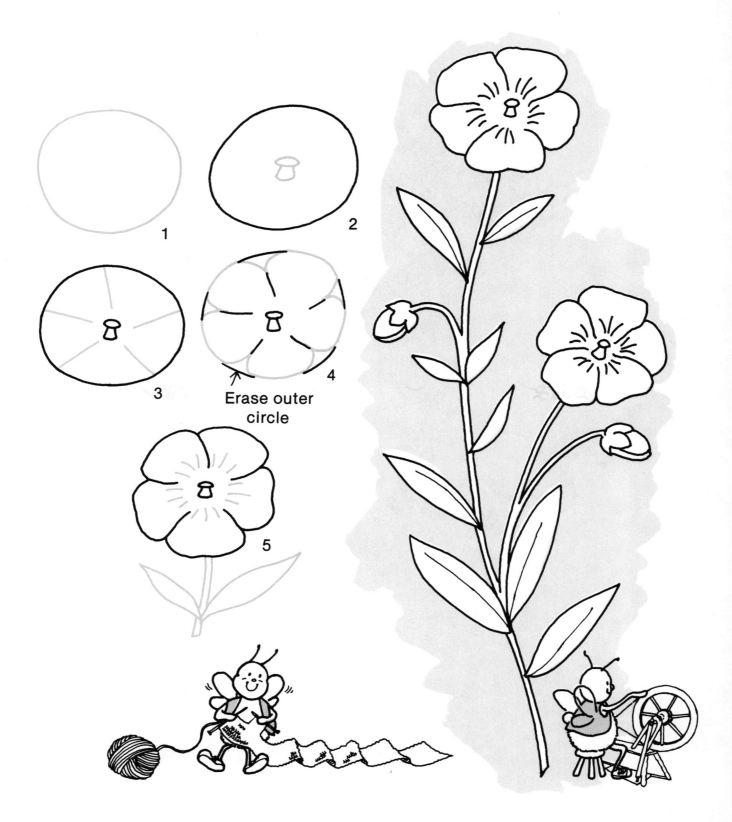

1

2

3

4

Erase outer circle

5

Buttercup

The buttercup is a bright yellow wild flower that adds a special glow to a flowering meadow. But be careful! Although it looks like a cup of delicious butter, the buttercup should never be eaten! It contains poison.

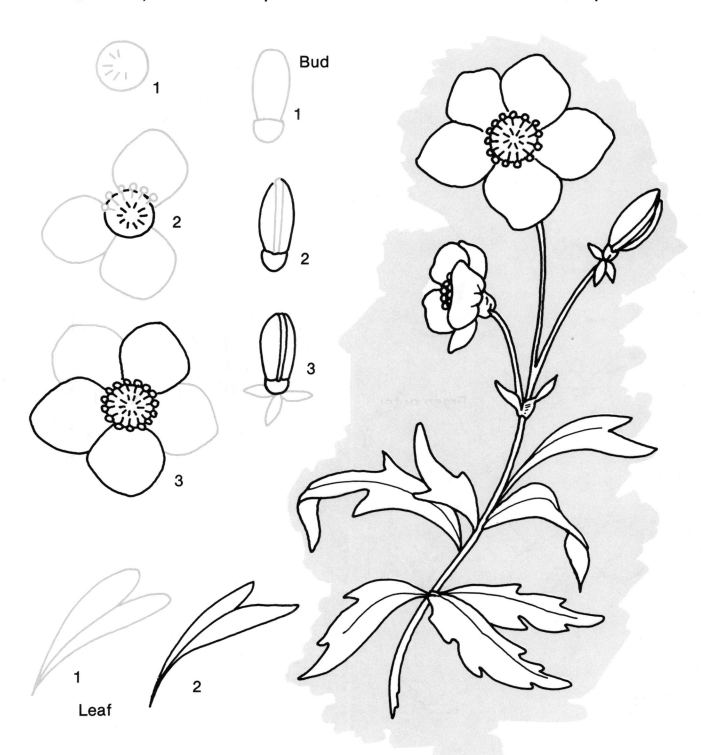

1

Bud

1

2

2

3

3

3

Leaf

1

2

Wild Strawberries

Wild strawberries can be found in meadows, woods, and fields. Each plant spreads by putting out a runner. The runner takes root and then produces new plants. Wild strawberries can be made into beverages, jellies, jams, and delicious desserts.

Blackberries

The blackberry is a shrub with arching shoots. The shoots take about a year to grow in length. During the second year, they bear fruits and flowers. Blackberries can also be made into a wide variety of dishes. Do you have a favorite recipe for blackberries?

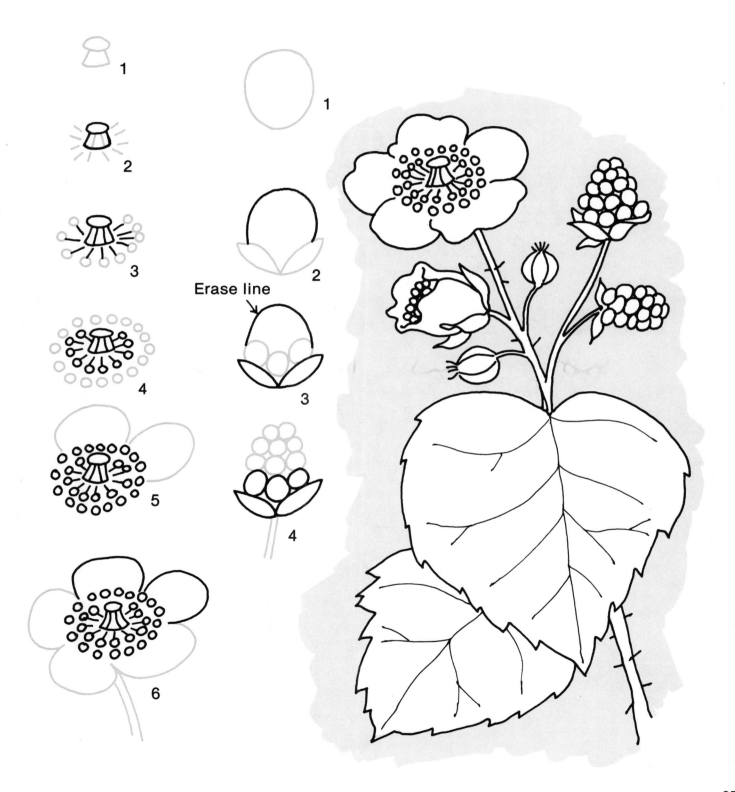

1

2

3

4

5

6

1

2

Erase line

3

4

White Water Lily

The water lily is an unusual flower—it moves with the sun! As the sun begins to set in the late afternoon, the flowers of the water lily begin to close. By nightfall they are completely submerged under water. Early in

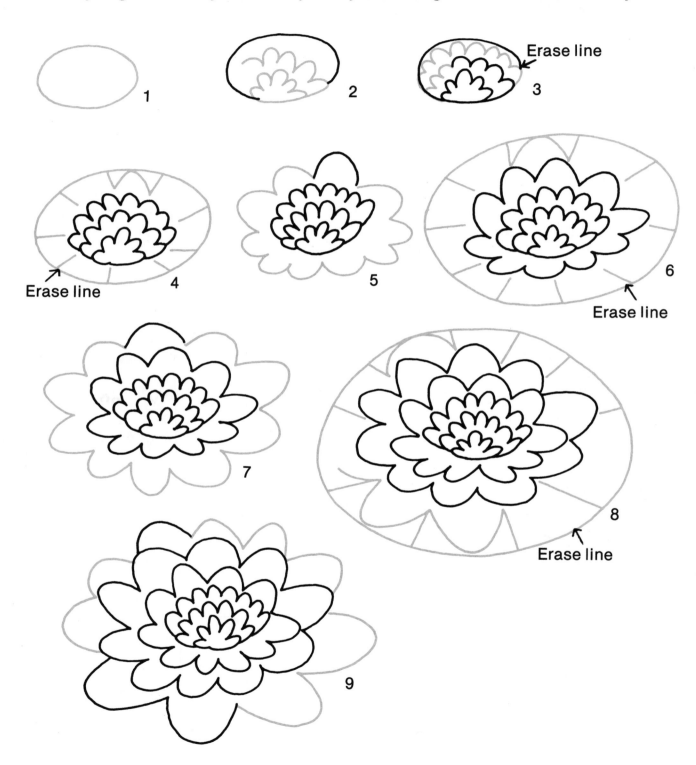

Erase line

1

2

Erase line   3

Erase line   4

5

6   Erase line

7

8   Erase line

9

the morning the closed blooms rise to the surface once again and open if the sun is shining. Facing east toward the sunrise, the water lily follows the sun's path all day. When evening comes the little flower faces west and bids farewell to the day!

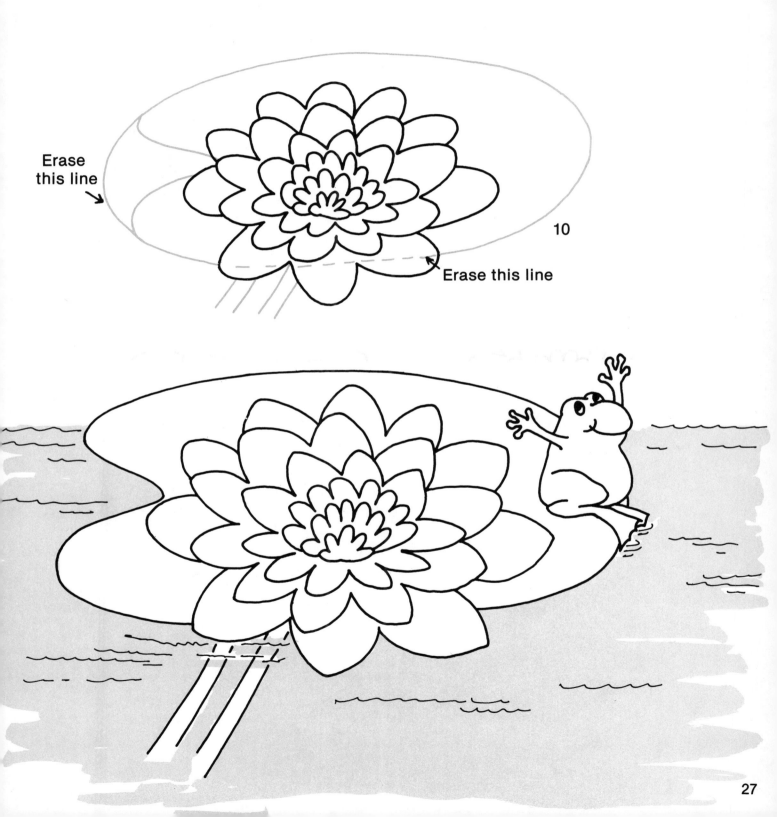

Erase this line

10

Erase this line

Prickly Pear

The prickly pear is a plant with flat, fleshy lobes, which may be smooth or prickly and which grow one on top of the other. Their beautiful red and yellow flowers decorate many a rock garden and their large berries can be eaten as fruit or used to make sweets.

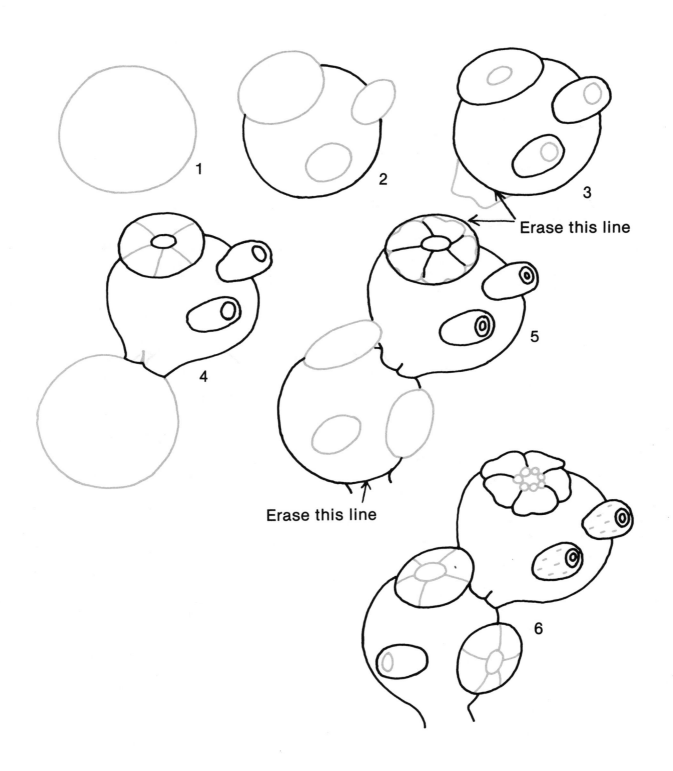

Erase this line

Erase this line

The prickly pear is a desert cactus, native to the dry climate of Mexico. Like other desert plants, it has adapted to the lack of water in its surroundings by storing large amounts of water in its fleshy tissue. And, like other desert plants, the prickly pear must use its water carefully —for the moisture taken in during the desert's brief rainy season must last for many hot, dry months!

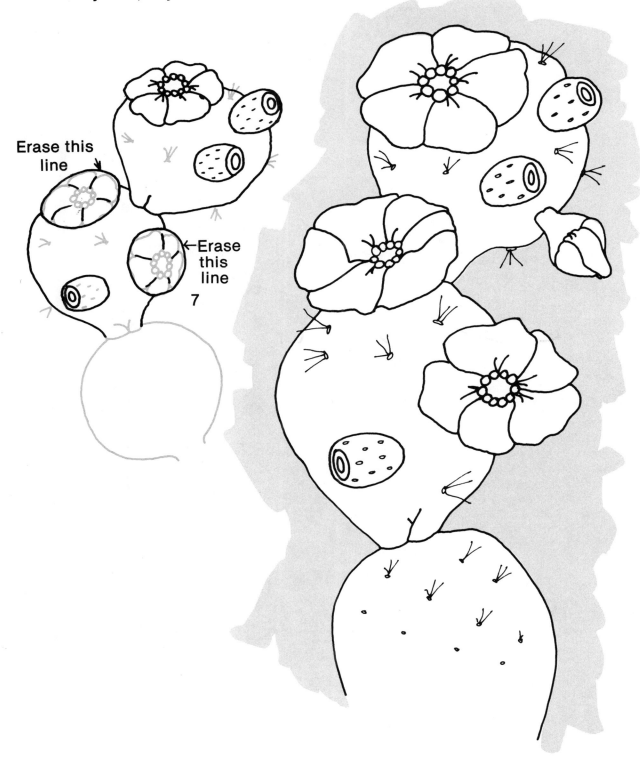

Erase this line

←Erase this line

7

Houseleek

The houseleek is a cactus plant that grows on cliffs, hillsides, and even on walls! Its tightly closed rosettes enable it to survive long periods of time without water. The houseleek often forms great clumps by means of side rosettes that can multiply and spread. During its flowering season, the houseleek develops a thick-leaved stem, topped by a cluster of greenish-yellow flowers.

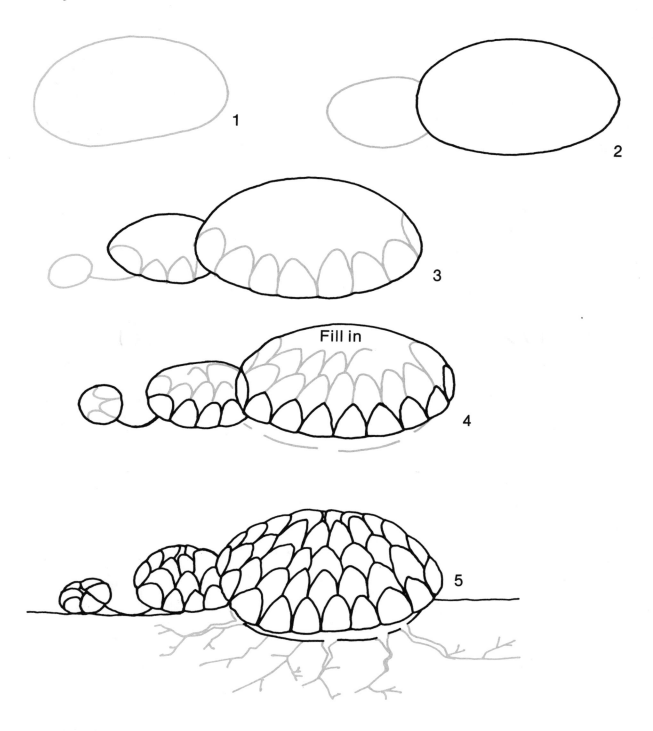

1

2

3

Fill in

4

5

1

2

3

4

The End